Edward E. Felder, Jr. MBA

"LET THEM

EAT CAKE"

Haters Gonna Hate, Bankers Gonna Deny

- You Build Wealth!

Strategic steps to secure funds to keep your business afloat and running!

To register for our online lending BootCamp or to purchase other books from us, titled: "It's money in the bank: 7 Insider Tips to Financing Any Small Biz" or "business credit made ridiculously simple" visit www.TheFundingGuy.com

ISBN: 978-0-9896798-5-5

Phone: 813 245 3293

Advance Praise

While sitting in Economics class, I pegged Eddie as my mentor. 25 years later he is more of a financial wiz then ever. If you truly want to master the play by play financing of your small business Let Them Eat is a MUST read. I easily find this book on par with that of Reginald Lewis the billionaire financier!

James Sutherland
Former Political & Economic Development Advisor to Congresswoman Donna Christensen

From the moment you begin reading Let Them Eat Cake you are immediately captivated by one of the most dynamic books written to this day. With a riveting array of stories and many laugh out loud moments, Edward Felder Jr. delivers a tangible and relevant guide to business success that makes you wonder why this book wasn't written sooner.

If you're looking for good humor, great knowledge, and a way to seize the day then this book is for you.

Brad & Jae Snell
Owners, Inspired By A Message TV Show

Exquisite storytelling with urban sensibilities. Edward breaks down stock broker talk into man-on-the-street stories. Armed with this info, the little guy can land a knockout blow.

Robert Kennedy III
President, LEEP Leadership Mentors

"Let Them Eat Cake" explains the reality that money is unlimited and so are the opportunities.

True genius is when complex concepts are explained in a simple way and this book is another example of Ed's gifts and mastery of cash flow.

I am all for anything that empowers a person, regardless of background or status, to become wealthy...and I am all for this book!

Jeff Ross
Founding Partner, K.E.G. Systems LLC

In a world where "common sense ain't so common", Felder's talent to break down intricate financial concepts to easily digestible parts is genius. Who gets business financing these days? YOU do once you've read THIS book.

Ed Warren
Partner, Mangrove Financial Group

Let Them Eat Cake is a power-punched, no holds-barred self examination that causes the end users to ask, how can I be what I seek?

Outstanding, Insightful, and extraordinarily helpful! Ed Felder, my friend and mentor has again produced a book with knowledge that every leader must know"

Sam Harris III
Real Estate Concierge, Financial Expert

Let Them Eat Cake gave me a better understanding about the principles of business funding. It's a witty, fantastic, playbook on how entrepreneurs seamlessly win business funding.

Beth Feagins, CSCS
MyFit 365.Com

I have found it difficult to put my IPad down. This book is next level and I am grateful for the information that will be beneficial to me as I move forward in 2017. Edward is brillant!!!! This book has changed my life in two weeks.

Connie L. S. Hall, M.Ed

Dedication

I am inspired by your determination.

You remind me of my Dad - who graduated as the number one ranked recruit in a class of 1,500, at the New York City Police Academy, after years of being denied entry into the academy.

I am inspired by your desire for greatness.

You remind me of my younger brother - who slept on park benches while in law school. Incredulously, your uncle ran away from home at 7 years of age, because he wanted to live a better life. Today he is chiefly credited for closing one of the largest mergers in TV history.

I am inspired by your passion to become an entrepreneur.

You remind me of a13-year-old me.

Surprisingly, days before I was expected to begin my high school career, I announced to my mother, guidance counselor, and principal, that I would be skipping high school & college and moving directly on to a top tier Business School namely Harvard, Yale or possibly Cal Berkeley.

It didn't matter that I wasn't a scholar or on their radar. I told myself it was just a matter of time, before they all came courting me. I wanted to become a top tier entrepreneur so bad, I could taste it.

Because you've inspired me to see the Can in those who believe they can't.
Because you've shared in my desire to help others Live a Better life.

*I dedicate **"Let Them Eat Cake"** to you, my amazing 16 year old son.*

Greatness is written all over you.

As you navigate toward your higher purpose, never lose your passion for pouring into others and inspiring them to reach their greater.

May God's riches blessing be upon you.

Edward E. Felder, III.
"Eddy"

Table of Contents

Foreword

I bought this book thinking he's seems like a nice enough guy, I'll give it a few pages. 125 pages and 14 chapters later, I went from causally reading to spellbound curled up, in my big chair.

I was blown away how the author brilliantly merged stories on Ali's historic victory over Foreman, tied 80-year- old Clara Peller's "Where's The Beef" commercial into a lending lesson, then highlighted how to avoid being like Wimpy (Mr. I' ll gladly Pay You on Tuesday For A Hamburger) when pitching your banker.

In short, "Let Them Eat Cake" is a masterpiece on winning Work Capital!

I was so captivated by "Let Them Eat Cake" I had The Funding Guy (Edward) on my nationally syndicated radio show five times.

This funding BluePrint is Worth Every Penny!

If you're anything like me, you'll find yourself laughing out loud all the way to the bank!

Dr. Anthony Mays, *Retired Military Commander,*
President, *Breakthrough Bible College and Theological Seminary*

Introduction

Word spread like wildfire, there was a maddening stampede; blacksmiths, seamstresses, builders and restaurateurs jawed and swung elbows violently, as thousands pressed their chilled faces against the frigid gold-plated palace gate. Although, they hoped to snag a glimpse of King Louis XVI, they fervently prayed they'd garner a brief audience with their Queen.

Just a few years earlier, she held a magnificent feast where she served the best of wines, the tastiest of cheese, and the warmest of bread to 50,000 adorning, upwardly mobile citizens. Everyone was made to feel as though they were part of the Queen's inner circle. Day turned into night, and night turned into day. It was a celebration overflowing with grandeur. No expense was spared, and no stomach left empty.

As the citizens angrily paced outside the palace gates, there was no longer any hint of the good life. The red carpet was rolled up, the bread was snatched off the table and the cheese, it simply melted. Nothing said life *of the party, or all you can eat,* gone were the remnants of that great feast. The overriding sentiment of those enjoying the good life, behind the iron gates was, "just make them go away."

Despite the lukewarm reception, all the enthusiastic entrepreneurs wanted to see and to be seen by her Majesty, the Queen. Each one of them hoped that they'd be the one invited to rub shoulders with the mighty Queen. They lined the street of the most opulent living quarters in all of Europe, "The Palace of Versailles."

Etiquette be damned!

Little kids were kicked to the curb, and the elderly, well they were knocked back and knocked down. Nobody checked on the less fortunate to make sure they were okay. Each imagined they'd be the one to capture the Queen's eye. For many clinging to the gate, this wasn't just a once in a lifetime opportunity, it was a matter of life and death.

The economy was in a horrific free-fall; everything that could go wrong, actually went terribly wrong!

Europe, once a cornucopia of prosperity had become a land of lack. Everything was spiraling out of control and Murphy's Law was in full effect.

- *Cottages on the hill, which formerly sold for a king's ransom, were now being auctioned off at City Hall for pennies on the dollar.*

- *Seasoned entrepreneurs couldn't score working capital to buy material or to bypass bread shortages.*

- *There was no funding to harvest what was left of their once vaulted crop.*

The *coup de grace* was an astronomical rise in bread prices. The cost of a loaf of bread skyrocketed to nearly a month's wages, a *month's wages!*

The most successful of entrepreneurs struggled with how they'd feed their families. This was particularly arduous, since the average family of three ate two pounds of bread per day. There was no stretching, tossing or baking of bread, stale crumbs were all that remained. The townspeople longed to provide for their families, yet despite their best efforts, they were forced to rely on small portions of grain and charity to survive. Grown men were moved to tears, nothing was more critical than getting their hands on some bread.

Every small biz owner hoped to pitch their novel business idea and their desire to eat. They reasoned they'd be unstoppable once they won the Queen's favor.

Merchants who were accused of hoarding bread were hung first and asked questions later. In the blink of an eye, the good life of wine and cheese reverted to bread crumbs and sips of salt water.

The shopkeepers, the farmers, the blacksmiths, the fabric of society - were distraught! They cried out desperately to the bankers, the money managers, and the aristocrats. Society's finest, inexplicably turned a blind eye and a deaf ear faster than you could say, "Spread the Wealth!"

With 2,000 fountains in her garden, 700 rooms, 400 marble sculptures, and auspicious ceilings that made Michelangelo's Sistine Chapel look like the finger painting of a toddler, Marie Antoinette had the royalty of Europe green with envy.

The commoners knew that the Monarchy, especially the Queen, (who frequently lavished her inner circle with extravagant gifts) had the means to dramatically improve their lot-in life.

After the hoping, the praying, and the wishing, the enfeebled entrepreneurs were convinced this would be their one shot to "EAT" again. Dressed in their Sunday best, they clutched the scrolls that contained their plans of business. A young architect hoped to share his dream of building an exquisite cottage on the hill to entertain dignitaries from afar. Another boasted how he'd franchise a bread company, where they would bake mouthwatering croissants and warm French bread, served with delectable soups & salads. He claimed, they'd be "to die for!"

In the midst of unprecedented suffering, word spread that the Queen would be making her appearance forthwith. The people were thrilled to lay eyes on their beloved Queen. This was their moment. Things were destined to change – or at least that was what they thought.

Enthusiastic chants of "long live the Queen!" Were explosive and relentless. Once the Queen heard their cry, the people reasoned, she'd do everything in her power to right the ship.

- *She would listen to their plans to prosper.*

- *Her Majesty would eradicate their pain.*

- *She'd help them eat.*

Why wouldn't she? She had the keys to the city and the combination to the vault. Each citizen quietly rejoiced thinking "*I'll be able to feed my family, grow my business, and possibly go international with my dreams!*"

Seemingly out of nowhere, the royal horns blared. The Queen whom we've subsequently come to know as Marie

Antoinette was spotted hastily traveling through the exuberant crowd in a shiny red, 1792 convertible Bentley coupe.

Oblivious to the suffering of the people, the Queen was rumored to have asked the question: "Why do these opportunist appear so needy, so destitute and so thin?" She continued, "They should want for nothing. Have they no class?"

Upon learning the fact that the citizens were crying for bread, Marie leaned her head out the sporty Bentley, and with the ferocity of a spurned tornado barked, "They have their filthy hands out again!"

If you were on those cold gray streets, you might have witnessed the Queen clinching her fists, while mean mugging the startled peasants. Undoubtedly you would have flinched, after noticing how her face violently screamed "idiot."

Angrily, Antoinette shifted her stunning four foot high hairdo, leaned into her Chief Credit Officer, and yelled, "These people have the audacity to air this foolishness in public." She twirled around and then she shouted …

- *Why are they on my Royal streets?*

- *Who gave them permission to enter my courts?*

- *Can we tax them anymore?"*

I can imagine the pompous Antoinette's face turning beet red, and her lips, her lips twisted like a pretzel at the very thought of being asked to "Spread The Wealth." (You know, sacrifice a little bread.) No longer able to contain her emotions; with the fury of a lioness protecting her cubs, she roared - *"They have their hands out crying over a lack of bread or lack of financing. I decree it is their fault."*

Really it is! *"No, I can't keep quiet about these dreamers, these vagabonds. No, I won't be sharing what's in my safe."*

In her mind, she questioned their loyalty. She angrily shouted, *"Why do they not make their own bread? I'd die, I'd die a thousand deaths, before yielding a morsel of bread to these ingrates."*

There was a quiet awkwardness, followed by the Queen blurting out, *"Enough of this foolishness! Enough of asking for handouts!"*

In the face of brutal poverty, the child prodigy who was born with a silver spoon in her mouth; the girl who was shipped from Austria to France to build a wealth alliance, callously declared:

"Let Them Eat Cake!"

"I said, Let Them Eat Cake!"

Rumor has it, the privileged few, the ultra-wealthy, those money managers in the crowd sporting huge cigars; those who received, dare I say it, a "government bailout," fervently nodded their approval of the Queen's blasted comments.

In the original French, this infamous quote is; "Qu'ils mangent de la brioche" translated it means:

"Let Them Eat Rich, Expensive, and Funny-Shaped, Yellow 'eggy' Buns."

Here's the thing, Marie couldn't just leave it at cake! Queenie had to make things worse by adding insult to injury, by basically saying;

> *"Hey poor people, I hear your cry. Really, I do! I've been exactly where you are. Never mind about the 50,000 people I served wine, cheese, and cake to at my wedding. I've got a marvelous, idea. Why don't you put your monies together, and order the tastiest, most expensive, cake in Europe? Oh look, here's the royal chef's business card. I'm certain he would love to hear from you. Toddles!"*

Three words pierce my soul after visiting what might have been the Queen's parting shots.

- *Condescending*

- *Dismissive*

- *Heartless*

As the French saying goes; "plus ça change, plus c'est la même chose." This translates as "The more things change, the more things stay the same.

Fast-forward 225 years. Many reading "Let Them Eat Cake" have found themselves knocking on their local banker's doors, saying *"Madame Lender - I too would like to eat, may I have some bread?"*

The sentiment of far too many Wall Street types, you know those executives working in the ivory towers downtown, or kicked back in the corner office in your local neighborhood branch, is one of oblivion and utter disregard.

One minute they're sweet-talking you out of your firstborn's checking account, the next, they toss a little attitude and sourdough in your direction. When you express a desire to score working capital or borrow just a little of what you've put into their coffers; they begin hemming and hawing like, Ebenezer Scrooge on Christmas Eve. To show there is no ill will, they offer you a shiny new stainless steel toaster!

Am I right?

Before you have the opportunity to make your compelling "I have a dream or why I need money pitch," they're already slamming the vault shut and disingenuously patting you on the back. Almost mockingly, they're saying, "We'll run it up the flag pole," while briskly escorting you out of their office.

- *Their facial expressions.*
- *The tonality in their voice.*
- *Their not-so-subtle innuendos.*
- *All blatantly screaming.*

"Let Them Eat Cake!"

"I said, Let Them Eat Cake!"

Contrary to the belief of many bankers, the vast majority of small business owners aren't drowning in debt. They're drowning in disappointment! Many of today's aristocrats – the esteemed bankers, the CEOs of Credit   Union Central - are what I like to call *"dream snatchers"* quick to do away with your funding request.

- *They block your calls.*

- *Classify your urgent emails as spam.*

- *Treat your emergency texts like day-old bread.*

Herein lies the problem: *'Wannapreneurs'* (You know who you are), you make it easy for wealthy bankers to serve us a little shortbread and think that what they've doled out is more than adequate. I realized that many of you are in a dark place, you feel like you let your family down. You regret ever opening your business. You kick yourself for ruining your credit or ever approaching that insensitive banker.

Those dark days are over. I declare today is your season for a financial breakthrough!

The period that began shortly after Marie Antoinette uttered her frigidly cruel words has been dubbed the 'Age of Enlightenment'. It was the beginning of an upheaval we now refer to as the French Revolution.

As history so aptly tells us, things didn't turn out too well for "The Cake Lady," or her husband, King Louis XVI, who called himself the "Most Magnificent." All that mattered to the Royal family was a legacy of magnificence. They dreamed of building an amazing life and expanding their borders. They hoped for a legacy that would make dignitaries and peasants throughout Europe green with envy.

However, because of their propensity to live high off the hog, along with an appetite for instant gratification, the kingdom's wealth withered and their legacy died!

Today, many of you have dreams of carving a brilliant legacy by:

- *Franchising your ideas.*

- *Expanding internationally.*

- *Leaving a healthy inheritance for your loved ones but your kingdom is in a crisis.*

In far too many cases, your dreams are nothing short of a house of cards on the brink of collapsing and you, my friend, are summarily deemed to be a little joker in banking circles.

> *"Failure is simply the opportunity to begin again, this time more intelligently.*
> *–Henry Ford, The great industrialist.*

Here's the thing, *"Let Them Eat Cake"* enlightens readers on how they can begin living a, renewed and fully reinvigorated life.

If you truly desire to win more than bits and pieces of chocolate brownies; it's time to unplug the easy bake oven, roll up your sleeves, and embrace the goodies disseminated within this enlightening manuscript.

When you pick up and live by the principles enshrined in this volume, you'll garner more than a measly slice of pie. You'll be gleefully escorted to your banker's vault and given carte blanche - to score all the capital your little house on the prairie requires.

- *How exciting would it be to go from just enough capital to fail, to being flush with working capital?*

- *What would it mean for your business?*

- *How amazing would it be to go from getting by on scraps, to dining on 7-course meals at the Tavern on The Green?*

Today, we're leveling the playing field; today is your shot at *"Enlightenment."*

I'm not saying you're going to live an enchanted life, full of grandeur and unquestioned privilege, neither am I saying that you'll be given unlimited rides on some mystical, magical carpet.

I can tell you, when you follow the tasty treats offered in this appetizing book, you'll have the opportunity to kick up your feet and smile in your banker's face, knowing you'll be gifted the tastiest cakes in the kingdom.

It's time for "your" breakthrough, it's time to eat!

"I have not failed. I've just found 10,000 ways that won't work." – Thomas Edison

"The Funding Guy"

CHAPTER I

Is it finger licking good?

I grew up in the South Bronx, in one of the worst housing projects in America, I was known as an outstanding athlete and a momma's boy.

That was my reputation, and I was proud of it. I'd slice and dice you up on the hardwood, and then bolt up nine flights of stairs to nestle under momma's wing; all I wanted to do was to treat her well.

While I was no Paula Deen or G. Garvin in the kitchen, I dreamed of baking momma the tastiest triple-decker birthday cake imaginable.

If I pulled off my cake shenanigans, (and that was a big if) I'd be a 12-year-old legend and she'd be ecstatic. For three consecutive weekends, when momma left for church, I'd sneak to the kitchen. I'd crank up the stove, grease the cake

1

pan, and then dump a load of milk, eggs and flour into a huge dish!

I'd shake up the pan, toss it in the oven and wait for my miracle to rise. For the first two weeks, my masterpiece turned out to be a master failure. With six days left before her huge surprise birthday bash, I felt just like the cake looked, a great big flop.

I was going half-crazy trying to figure out what I'd done wrong. I told myself that since life is handing me lemons, I'd throw them in the pan and make a lemon-flavored cake, (hey, I was just a kid.)

After interviewing several of the area master chefs – from a guy who owned a hot dog stand, to a little girl who claimed she knew all there was to know about making cakes by watching Maria on Sesame Street; I had a pretty good handle on what I'd done wrong. Everything!

Although, I was no Chef Boyardee in the kitchen, I felt like round three would be a cake walk. Why not? If what my coaches told me proved correct, this was almost going to be too easy! On the D-Day, 30 minutes before the party kicked off, I stuck my chest out and declared that I'd made the cake of all cakes!

Lighthearted laughs filled the room. I'm sure my siblings had a cake or two stashed in a brown paper bag - just in case things turned out to be *'far messier than mouthwatering'*. There were multiple jokes about the cake being up to par, and it being down and out. Despite the ungodly ribbing, I knew without a shadow of a doubt that I had nailed a hole in one.

What they didn't know was that; I had made a master shift, and there wasn't anything mediocre about my cooking or baking skills that time around. I vowed to play by the rules and adhere to the "*expert's advice*" meticulously.

There wasn't any improvising or haphazard tossing of ingredients in the bowl this time around. There was no debate about what went in first - the chicken, the egg, or the milk. Nothing was freelance! There were no following the letter of the law shenanigans this time. I was fully committed and totally immersed in the process, I was transparent!

Every ounce of cake mix, every nanosecond on the blender, every drip of Deer Park Water - followed the exact script outlined by my coaches.

Rather than just tossing what I'd already predetermined was a masterpiece into the oven (which was my prior modus operandi,) I executed what the little girl next door had coined the **"Oh, Taste and See Method."**

My initial reaction was "this kid's been chewing on too many colored skittles." Then it hit me like a ton of bricks, I quietly realized it couldn't be any worse than the shotgun method, I'd invested so heavily in.

I'd put a shot of this, dump a shot of that, and hoped everything tasted okay, once I pulled the cake out the oven.

"DaDAAA!"

No harm, no foul - or at least that's what I'd thought before sampling the product. Ouch!

The chef next door had informed me that it was "*prudent*" for me to taste the mix before tossing it in the oven. In her words, "I couldn't just dive in, No!!!"

My actions had to be more "refined." There was, as she said, "*an Art to Tasting*" – even a science.

Step 1

Thoroughly scrub all ten fingers.

Step 2

Slightly dip index finger in said cake mix, then quickly swirl it around the edge of the bowl three times.

Step 3

Place finger in mouth to ensure product met or exceeded the preordained quality standard. Interpretation - my blend was no longer tart.

Step 4

If it passed mustard (the initial taste test), I was instructed to give the room a quick glance, to ensure no

one was looking, then carefully dip my head, and lick the remnants of the mix left in the bowl.

Hey, don't judge me! I was 12, and fully committed.

Right!

Step 5

Dash to the mirror to ensure the cream all over my face, on my sleeves and lingering on my nose was vaporized. Once, the evidence was gone; no one would be the wiser. Although slightly embarrassing, I like to think, I was simply doing my job!

My colleagues in the banking community might call it my "due diligence." After trying again, to my surprise, the cake mix was magically delicious. I mean, it was so much more than I'd hoped. Because I'd tested, I'd tasted, and I'd reviewed the batter before throwing it in the oven, I was confident that once cooked, it would be the best cake momma ever had. I was pretty darn sure that I'd exceeded everyone's wildest expectations.

I didn't want to disappoint myself, more importantly, I hated the idea of falling flat on my face, delivering a cake that was half-baked, bitter, or just downright crummy. I didn't want to be exposed as a hack, I wanted unfettered access to the kitchen in the future. This was my chance. So I continued, with a second round of due diligence, which called for me to liberate the silver prongs of any residue. After licking both silver prongs free of all cream, I knew that without question, my cake was *"Finger Licking Good!"*

By the time I stood in front of the committee of six - the little girl next door, my aunties, and my cynical sisters - I could unequivocally proclaim that I'd made a cake that was supercalifragilisticexpialidocious! I was supremely confident, I'd be the talk of the town.

I only wanted to please momma. I didn't have the luxury of failing forward another day. I was on the clock, and it was ticking loud and clear. As my mom wrapped her fingers around the razor sharp Ginsu Knife and sliced into the cake, our eyes momentarily locked. I was infused with nervous energy. I was going half-insane, praying her initial taste brought an endless smile, rather than a call for a tall glass of milk. The wide-eyed expression on her face confessed without words: she was intoxicated by the rich, moist taste.

Bam!!! At that very moment, I knew I had her, hook, line, and sinker. She grabbed me by my waist, spun me around, and jubilantly said 'the cake was divine'. I wanted to cry in her arms, but I puffed out my meager little chest instead.

I'd spent my last dime (well, I actually spent my big sister Lynnette's last dime) but it was all worth it. My due diligence and obsession with getting it right paid off big time. I was lauded as king for a day, saluted with "I can't believe you pulled it off" high fives and outfitted with an oversized chef's apron that read "Finger Licking Good!"

I was stoked, everything broke according to plan. The sky was the limit, at least in my little mind. I envisioned myself being interviewed on "Live with Regis and Kathie Lee," and Regis pleading with me for my recipe like it was the secret formula for Coca-Cola.

I am thoroughly convinced that had I stayed in the cake business, rather than branching off to lemonade stands and banking, I would have been a snack food maven, on par with Little Debbie, Ms. Fields, and Ben & Jerry.

I would easily rival Starbucks, Apple, and Nike for the title of "Most Beloved Brand!" I'd be enshrined in the Bakers Hall of Fame. (Yes, it exists in Hutchinson, Minnesota). During my acceptance speech, I'd share how my imperfect pass to stardom was made possible by having three bites of the apple. I would tell the tale of how I failed miserably on my first two attempts at baking the cake - and only nailed it after learning the value of tasting my batter before the heat was on.

Today, as a 25-year lending executive, arguably the most powerful piece of advice I have received - outside of Mark Cuban urging me to;

> *"Work like there is someone working*
> *twenty-four hours a day to take it all away*
> *from you." – Mark Cuban*

Came from the little girl next door - who implored me to embrace the *"Oh, Taste and See Method."* Because of her, I was hailed as a master chef, on the biggest stage of my life. I was terrified of ruining mom's big event by delivering a nondescript, cardboard tasting lemon of a cake. If not for my constant determination to check and

7

double check my cake mix, the cake and I would have been a tragedy waiting in the wings.

Today, many business owners on the precipice of greatness have frighteningly picked right up where I left off as a 12-year-old aspiring baker. By that I mean, they bear a striking resemblance to the knucklehead kid, who dashed off haphazardly, vowing to quickly build an amazing cake after succumbing to a little voice in his head.

A story was told of an exuberant young intern from Harvard beating the hot pavement on Wall Street for a summer internship.

Upon exiting the New York City subway for the first time and staring up at the sky, he was overwhelmed by the sheer height and number of skyscrapers towering above him. Immediately, he felt like the proverbial fish out of water. Nothing in his hometown of Kansas was as daunting as the maddening stampede of seemingly hostile executives sporting Kenneth Cole shoes and a bad attitude, blazing a trail directly toward him, at a race horse pace. He took a deep breath, and coaxed himself into thinking that he was ready for the city. He had taken all of three steps before he heard a panicked voice shout, "Stop! Stand still! If you take one more step, a brick will come crashing down and it'll kill you." He thought this was ridiculous, but stopped nonetheless. A nanosecond later, a massive cinderblock smashed into the cement and missed him by a centimeter. Bewildered, the intern bolted from the vicinity. As the sprinting boy neared a blind corner, he again heard the voice shout: "Stop! Stand still! If you take another step you'll be killed!" The boy immediately threw up his hands and stopped on a dime. As he did, a gunman came blazing out of a small community bank. Flying bullets ricocheted everywhere. Hiding in plain sight he escaped by a hair!

Though chilling, he thought wow, this is pretty darn amazing. He thanked his lucky stars, and then had the "*bright idea*" of walking across a ridiculously busy intersection with both eyes shut.

Why shouldn't I? He thought.

I have a guardian angel looking out for me at every turn, the newly christened New Yorker thought. Without taking a deep breath, he blindly and nonchalantly crossed the street in rush hour traffic, cheerfully humming skip, skip, and skip to my Lou.

One step, two steps, ten steps, twenty-five steps - this was a cinch! There was barely a horn blaring. It was as if he was venturing out on a lazy Sunday morning where time and traffic stood still for him. Steps 26, 27, 28, and 29. It seemed as if he was skating on ice. The thrill of doing the unthinkable made the hair on his neck stand up. I've gotta be destined for greatness he thought. Wall Street will be my canvass for a blank check, the intern boasted to himself.

As he planted his left foot on what he thought was the curb on the opposite end of the street, the ground beneath him disappeared, and he plunged into the air. With arms flailing and feet swinging wildly, the young intern tried to slow the most terrifying plummet imaginable.

Two questions quickly pierced his thick skull:

1. Who the hell left the manhole open?

2. Where the heck was his guardian angel?

The intern's $500 Oxford wingtip shoes were useless in stopping his descent into the dark abyss. His polished fingertips were ripped from his blistered fingers while trying to slow his fall. He contorted his body, readying for a cataclysmic crash. It was all of no use, he landed on his back, shattering his vertebrae. He shrieked in agony! He'd never known such horrendous pain.

Like most people immediately after an accident, he vowed this was the last time he did something so fool-hearted and reckless. Never again would he take off blindly. He opened his eyes and saw a bright blue sky and the most amazing cloud smiling down on him.

He wondered aloud whether he was in heaven, but quickly summarized it couldn't be heaven: as he was in such excruciating pain. Adrenaline rushed through his mangled body. He tried gripping the slippery walls to climb out of his godforsaken pit, only to find out that he'd grabbed a fistful of white linen sheets.

That's when it hit him, he wasn't caught up in a deep hole. He was actually in his own bed. The dreaded fall he experienced, well it was only in his dreams.

It was all a frightening nightmare!

Like so many make-believe chefs, and Wall Street interns, today's aspiring entrepreneurs, in their haste to rake in the big score, are still childlike in their approach. On the biggest stage of their lives, they're blindly following the little voices in their head telling them to rush forward without conducting the slightest bit of due diligence.

This faux pas can be winked at when you're an anxious 12-year-old pretend chef, looking to impress your mom with a red velvet cake. However, when you're locking down a lucrative contract, and you require the blessing of a skeptical lender; one seemingly inconsequential misstep, like neglecting to check your credit prior to submitting your request, can have you up a creek without a paddle, stuck in sand in a rising tide or behind the eight ball. Well, you get the point!

The witty British statistician Sir Claus Moser once told a crowd of academic know-it-alls, something that'll last a life time;

> *"Education costs money: but then so does ignorance."- Sir Claus Moser.*

Here's the thing, intentional or otherwise, the lack of due diligence is costing you money and leaving a bitter imprint on your banker.

In less than a New York minute, you'll be summarily dismissed, and the funding pitch, well it'll be ditched like a spoiled slice of upside down cake.

The amazing thing is that; aspiring entrepreneurs can come off as burgeoning rock stars, ready to rip the runway by simply looking before they leap.

Wealth Principle # 1

It's You VS. You
Give 10,001% during preparation. Be so polished that
your haters join your band and sing your praises.

In the banking world, unlike the world I resided in as a 12-year-old kid, you never get a second or third chance to make a first impression. Lenders no longer wait around for you to get your mix together, no one does that. They fully expect you to have a mouthwatering finished product out the box. They expect your pitch to be *Finger Licking Good*! They're looking for game-changers, not day old excuses and do over requests.

Rather than sprinting to an amazing financial future where everything is signed, sealed and perfectly delivered to Banker X, we engage in child's play when it comes to our credit.

The debt management strategy we employ is eerily similar to a fairy tale joyfully recited by most four-year-olds. You know it, it begins with chants of; "Run, run, as fast as you can - you can't catch me, I'm the Ginger Bread Man." It's cute, it's catchy, and to be completely honest, I can see how it caught on.

However, you're only fooling or outfoxing yourself kinda like, the kiddie cook, if you are expecting a gourmet meal that is fit for a real king.

Rather than *Supercalifragilisticexpialidocious*, they're inviting you to exit stage left. Instead of *Fingering Licking Good* cheers, they're readying to shoot you the finger!

We trick ourselves into thinking those people, those bankers don't want to lend us money anyway. Because of this mindset, we retreat and fall back on a tried and true strategy: ***Hear No Evil, See No Evil, and Do No Evil!***

- *Look before you leap?*

- *Take corrective action?*

- *Live below your financial means?*

Nope! None of those financially prudent actions are in the cards. We hold onto the notion that our funding will somehow miraculously pan out perfectly like a beautifully sculptured, well planned cake.

Really?

Hiding your head in the sand simply won't fix the problem, or sweeten the taste. Unless you're satisfied with mere breadcrumbs, you have to decisively make a choice to move ahead.

> *"We cannot solve our problems with the same thinking we used when we created them."*
> *- Albert Einstein.*

If you're sick and tired of grasping at straws and nibbling around the perimeter of success and you're ready to bathe in the funding success that has eluded you over time, visiting credit rating sites, such as CreditKarma.com (which is completely free) and adhering to the suggested credit adjustments will make you appear freaking amazing on paper.

You'll go from a vagabond in lending circles to winning multiple invites at your banker's welcome table.

> *"Two roads diverged in a wood, and I - I took the one less traveled by, and that has made all the difference."*
> *– Robert Frost.*

If you 'Stop! Stand still' - take the road less traveled, by that I mean, look before you leap; undoubtedly you'll go from skipping to your Lou and skating on thin ice, to a life on the easy street.

There'll be no more sliding down slippery slopes, struggling blindly in the midst of a terrible storm, or hearing bitter denials; since you now have the recipe to create a request that is unequivocally, *Finger Licking Good!*

The Funding Lounge

1. What 'Aha' moment did you gather from Chapter One?

_____

_____

_____

_____

2. How has hiding your head in the sand negatively impacted your funding and business growth?

_____

_____

_____

_____

3. What changes are you planning to make in the next 9 days, 9 weeks and 9 months, that will make your personal credit scores Finger Licking Good?

a. What actions will be taken in the next 9 days?

_____

_____

_____

_____

b. What results would you like to see in 9 weeks?

_____

_____

_____

_____

c. Where do you see your business and potential for financing in 9 months?

_____

_____

_____

_____

"Any intelligent fool can make things bigger, more complex, and more violent. It takes a touch of genius—and a lot of courage—to move in the opposite direction."
- E.F. Schumacher

CHAPTER II

Sweeten the pot

He had just been slapped in the face with such venom you'd swear his cheekbone was shattered and he'd had a few teeth dislodged. Despite the heinous punch he'd just absorbed, he wore a Cheshire's grin on his swollen face. Perhaps, he'd lost and regained consciousness while stumbling on his feet?

If you figured he'd try running away from the pain, you'd be sadly mistaken. He just stood, stared and smiled a lot. It was as if he was saying, I'm good! No really I'm good! Don't cry for me Argentina! While the astonished bystanders were wincing at the pain he'd just received, he was most likely thinking:

> *"I'd wrestled with an alligator, I tussled*
> *with a whale; I handcuffed lightning,*
> *thrown thunder in jail; only last week, I*
> *murdered a rock, injured a stone,*

> *hospitalized a brick; I'm so mean I make*
> *medicine sick."*
> *– Muhammad Ali*

It was completely baffling, The loudmouth who'd called himself pretty, who's joke goes like; *"It's hard to be humble when you're as great as I am,"* appeared inches and moments away from being hospitalized by the monstrous haymakers that were lighting up his liver, crushing his larynx, and cutting off his lateral movement. In all honesty, nothing was pretty about the walloping he was being administered. Was this poetic justice?

Days earlier, he had quipped, *"If you ever dreamed of beating me in your sleep, you'd better wake up and apologize to me."* Gone were his one-liners about "floating like a butterfly and stinging like a bee." His facial expression begged for a genie in a bottle, to grant his escape, from what could only be described as a festering hornet's nest.

In the eyes of the 60,000 fans collectively holding their breaths, it appeared Ali was shadow boxing, while the bruiser was carving up Ali, and beating him to pulp.

His fans screamed. "Ali Bomaye! Ali Bomaye!" "Kill him Ali! Kill him Ali!" It was all a pipe dream. They prayed Ali wasn't plowed into the first row. If things didn't change quickly, Ali's flesh, blood, and what was left of his mauled body, would be permanently entwined with the ropes he'd been clinging to, for dear life!

There was no defying the odds, or chance at a truce! Ali had gone too far with his theatrics, unleashing a brutal tongue lashing against the scorned Goliath. No sooner than the announcer screamed *"Are you ready to Rummmmmmbble?"* The melee dubbed, "The Rumble in the Jungle" seemed destined for a new headline - "Murder on The Orient Express!" There would be no whodunit twist or teasing. The culprit, George Foreman, was big, bold, and unabashed about smashing the mouth of the 'loud mouth'.

If things went according to his plan, Ali would never don another pair of gloves, mittens, or socks.

Boxing aficionados, including many of Ali's closest allies like 'The Fight Doctor' Ferdie Pacheco and legendary fight announcer Howard Cosell pleaded with Ali to walk away, simply walk away - from the behemoth billed as the "The Baddest Man on the Planet!"

After witnessing Foreman (40-0, 37 knockouts) spank undefeated heavyweight champ, Joe Frazier like he stole something expensive; (no scratch that) something priceless; then toss the #1 challenger, Ken Norton, Jr., around like a slinky down a steep flight of stairs, they simply wanted Ali to avoid Foreman's grilling.

In their minds, it was a forgone conclusion, Ali would be ridiculed, ripped to shreds, and possibly laid to rest; especially, if Foreman held true to his promise to kill someone in the ring; namely Ali. Foreman was no snake oil salesman, he truly planned to maim the disrespectful Muhammad Ali. That bout wasn't business, it was personal.

More than ever, Ali's brain-trust were convinced that Ali had no business putting his hat in the ring.

- *Ali wasn't strong enough to withstand Foreman's ungodly arsenal of body blows.*

- *Ali was too slow to avoid the cataclysmic cannons Foreman would bequeath, Ali's kidneys.*

- *Ali wasn't nimble enough to dance the right way.*

Perhaps, he was no longer wise enough either. They'd wished like hell, that Ali steered clear of the Woolly Mammoth.

Did Ali know the fury he had aroused in the beast? Was he oblivious of the pain that would be afflicted upon him by Foreman? Rumors swirled, that Ali had a secret strategy that would overcome and outwit Foreman. Hmm!

Was there a method to Ali's madness? Was this simply more Ali's gamesmanship or pontificating?

Obviously not!

In the blink of an eye, Foreman buried a left hook deep into Ali's liver, Ali winced and a single tear, betrayed Ali; signaling to Foreman, that he was indeed putting a whopping of epic proportion on Ali. Foreman was no longer chasing waterfalls, true to his word, he was looking to bury Ali.

A series of devastating uppercuts, followed by, a stone fist to Ali's temple, seemingly, wobbled the head, heart, and will of Ali. Ali was being baptized in a sea of unforgiving kidney punches. Would the bout be mercifully halted? Ali's famous boxing trainer surely had the white towel within reach. Why wouldn't the stubborn Ali stay off the ropes?

Simply stay off the ropes!

Did Ali take the fight because he was still reveling in his old press clippings? Would the ropes be sturdy enough, to keep Ali from landing in Cosell's lap?

There was no place to escape. The onslaught wouldn't stop. It was constant, and severe!

Ali's corner implored him to dance. Just dance!

After one particularly vicious barrage of blows in the 6th round, Ali toiled to eke out, "George, George they told me you could punch like Joe Louis, is that the best that you have?" After a brief pause, he continued his incessant teasing by saying, "Is that the best you can do?"

Foreman looked frozen and lost - as if he was searching for a lighthouse, miles and miles away.

Was Ali really egging on the champ?

While it appeared Ali had gone half crazy, Ali was flawlessly orchestrating one of the most masterful fight plans offered up by an inherent underdog.

Albeit it was painful!

Wealth Principle # 2

Outwork your disbelief!
Pain is simply a temporary testing ground.

If you looked in Ali's eyes, they told you he was holding all the cards! If you'd stared too long, they'd most likely say please don't judge me.

In The Art of War, Sun Tzu, the brilliant military strategist, wrote:

> *"Victorious warriors win first and then go
> to war, while defeated warriors go to war
> first and then seek to win." – Sun Tzu*

From the way things were playing out, Ali was the defeated warrior - playing checkers, while Foreman was the mercenary playing chess. Despite the painfully obvious staring him square in the face:

- *There would be no White Towels Thrown In.*

- *No extending an invitation for the Fat Lady to sing.*

- *No Roberto Duran like cries of No Mas! No Mas!*

While the "reputed experts" at ringside believed the face painting George was issuing, was the beginning of the end; in Ali's mind, Ali was Michelangelo on the verge of putting the finishing touches on a masterpiece.

Although his body hinted at being an insurgent, he incredulously, doubled down on his foolhardy bet, by seemingly laying on the ropes, at that instance. His world renowned trainer, Angelo Dundee, cried Ali no more sacrifice. No more pain. Dundee, couldn't stomach the thought of Ali, dying on the ropes.

In the blink of an eye, it was all over!

Ali blitzed Foreman with a devastating left hook, followed by a morbid right, and that dropped the big bad wolf. It was as if Ali was a phoenix rising from the ashes! With apologies to the actor in the *'Dos Equis'* beer commercial, Ali whirled around and ushered a defiant stare that said, *"I Am The Most Amazing Man In The World."*

There was a deafening silence, followed by a euphoric cry of 60,000 cheering fans, who exploded into the aisles as Foreman's lower lip and bruised ego ricocheted off the canvass. The champ was definitely back!

Although, he'd been told a thousand times he'd never win, he wasn't good enough, and his legacy would be permanently tarnished if he took the fight, Ali did the unthinkable. He turned an inherent weakness into the victory of a lifetime. He'd turned lemon into lemonade! His unmistakable swagger was back.

A wide-eyed Ali defiantly glared at the throng of toxic reporters, who he counted amongst the nonbelievers; and jubilantly shouted:

> *"I am a scholar of boxing! I'm still the greatest of all times. Never again defeat me, never again say that I'm going to be defeated, and never again make me the underdog!"*
> *– Ali.*

On the biggest stage of his life, with an estimated worldwide TV audience of nearly a billion people, Ali delivered an Oscar-worthy thriller and it was truly something special. You're probably saying to yourself, how is Ali's victory 40 years ago going to help me win desperately needed funding today, tomorrow or the day after?

Stick here with me!

While smitten by Ali's bravado - the indisputable truth is that Ali's heroic, "Rumble in the Jungle" did more than simply inspire underdog fighters.

Hands down, the Ali story is a brilliant metaphor, stacked with teas leaves, if traced, will teach you to win loads of funding from the most conservative of lenders, even if you're sporting spotty or God-awful credit. I thought, why aren't more emerging entrepreneurs with soiled credit emulating the champ rather than chasing unforgiving bankers on bent knees?

The Ali way says, when you're facing insurmountable odds, when you're up against the ropes, entrepreneurs seeking funding no longer have to throw their hands up or cry, no mas no mas!

It tells you, although you have an inherent weakness, blemished personal credit, you no longer have to tap dance, tap out or throw in the towel. It says being bold, radical, and thinking outside the box, will be handsomely rewarded. It warns you, that while on your funding expedition, you'll likely encounter ringside experts–underwriters–crying bloody murder, pointing fingers claiming your:

- *Late pays.*
- *No pays.*
- *Plethora of promises to gladly pay on Tuesday.*

Will haunt you for a lifetime.

In the midst of their loud barking, the Ali way says, keep fighting on. Ali's unforgettable victory tells the credit challenged, they too can turn lemon into lemonade, by *Sweetening the Pot!*

Wealth Principle # 3

Earn it!
The hustle can't be bequeath!

In Ali's case, the sweetener was lying on the ropes and unveiling a brilliant new tactic, coined "the Rope-A-Dope!" It was so beautifully executed, that by the end of the bout, the naysayers no longer talked about Ali's lack of strength, his age or his dwindling speed. They simply marveled at his ability to pivot and weather the storm.

For aspiring entrepreneurs with battered and bruised credit, a brilliant, albeit radical way to *Sweeten the Pot* or bury the bitter taste of stinging loan denials; is to become laser-focused on creating a **Business Credit Profile.**

- *Radical? Yes.*

- *Unheralded? Not so much!*

- *Effective? Highly!*

No, I'm not suffering from delusions of grandeur, neither am I telling you that you'll be able to turn water into wine. What I am telling you, in Ali-speak is that; it's possible to achieve what many think of as impossible.

What I am poignantly sharing, is that for years, savvy entrepreneurs like The Donald of Taj Mahal Casio, and Robert Kiyosaki of Rich Dad Poor Dad fortune, have been successful in getting lenders to shift their focus away from their multiple bankruptcies and foreclosures, while converting them into raving fans.

RIGHT NOW . . . you're probably thinking, this hokey pokey strategy is simply reserved for the rich and famous. If you thought that, you'd be sadly mistaken. The beauty of Business Credit is that it doesn't require you to have pristine personal credit. In fact in 99% of funding, your personal credit isn't pulled, your social security number isn't requested, and your litany of credit faux pas aren't looked at, much less splattered in your face.

Is that sweet or what?

Rather than asking you to bow out gracefully because of your charred personal credit, most times lenders are jubilantly offering up the keys to the vault, (bestowing car leases, business credit cards, and unsecured lines of credit) to you. When it comes to business credit, you're no longer fighting with one hand tied behind your back due to prior indiscretions. As a matter of fact, you can scrap everything you thought you "knew" about FICO and personal credit scores.

While 97% of business owners are fixated on fighting the good fight - chasing a 700 credit score - you'll be shocked to learn that your personal FICO doesn't amount to a hill of beans when it comes to crafting a polished *Business Credit Profile*. While personal FICO scores range from

300 to 850, the business credit matrix is tallied on a scoring system where a max score is simply 100.

The 800-pound gorilla in the world of Business Credit is Dun & Bradstreet, known as DnB. DnB scoring modular is called PayDex. A 0-15 PayDex score is considered quite horrendous, while a rating from 80 to 100 is universally accepted as par excellence. Dun & Bradstreet focuses primarily on how a business interacts with vendors and other suppliers.

Psst…quick sidebar! Please know that there is a science to winning Business Credit. You can't simply dance around wildly slinging credit applications at every institution and expect a windfall from heaven. Once you have launched your **Business Credit Profile** adequately, you'll find bankers ecstatic about breaking bread with you. Believe it or not, in as little as 90 days you can have a powerful business credit score.

I can read your mind! I know what you're thinking!

You're saying, you're tired of bowing out gracefully, due to shaky credit. You're thinking, will this business credit really elevate my chances of winning growth capital? In a word, Yes!

Philosopher Isaac Asimov, who Ali greatly admired, once remarkably said;

> *"In life, unlike chess, the game continues*
> *after checkmate."*
> *- Isaac Asimov.*

In other words, rather than dancing with the devil when you're caught between a rock and hard place, when you're notified your personal scores are too charred to be lent to; the Ali way says that you can shake up the world by showcasing a shiny new Business Credit Profile.

Business Credit is an amazing sweetener. It turns a blind eye toward your smorgasbord of personal credit issues. It's like the good old Statue of Liberty, upon which this inscription rests;

> *"Give Me your Tired, your Poor, your Huddled Masses Yearning to Breathe Free."*

Similarly, Business Credit takes the downtrodden and puts them in a position that leave lenders in awe.

The beauty of Business Credit is that, in most cases you don't have to explain away an ill-advised short sale, or call in the cavalry to prove a parking ticket that is listed as a judgment on your personal credit, was never yours in the first place.

In 99.99% of cases when seeking Business Credit, you simply supply your Duns Number, and your properly recorded Federal Tax Identification Number, and you're off to see the wizard of working capital! In that rare instance a creditor decides they want to pull your much maligned personal credit, you can gracefully pull out your Duns Number as if they were - A Black Card and say, *"Never again defeat me, never again say that I'm going to be defeated, and never again make me the underdog!"*

31

Wealth Principle # 4

Own Relentless!
Almost doesn't count.

Although, many of the savvier entrepreneurs refer to Business Credit as liquid gold, I prefer to think of it as liquid cake or a giant smoothie!

Get this!

If you were to simply toss a few bitter lemons in your Magic Bullet or Nutri Ninja, along with a pinch of Deer Park Water, it would not be a delicious mouthwatering smoothie, am I right?

Aha, but if you were so inclined to sweeten the drink by adding say, a little mango, a dozen fresh strawberries, a dab of honey, along with a pinch of kiwi, papaya and a banana . . . you'd be lauded as the king of Smoothie King. Once you've *Sweetened the Pot*, there'll be no more talk about bitter lemons, prior failures, or bowing out gracefully. All eyes and thoughts will be on serving you the best of the best. If you're able to properly establish an amazing Business Credit Profile, and that's a big "if" for all intent and purpose, you'll be akin to Ali, chilling in the catbird seat.

Although you'll still have a sprinkle of nonbelievers ringside crying:

- *You're in over your head.*

- *You're past your prime.*

- *Go on ahead and throw in the towel.*

You'll just stop, stare and break out in a Cheshire's grin, knowing you're a financial champ who'll never again be defeated, or boxed into a corner; Since your sweetener will have lenders floating like a butterfly; and greeting you on bended knees!

Wealth Principle # 5

A Dream without the Fight
Is like Shadow Boxing in the Dark
It's ridiculous!

Without the fight, the sweat and blood, the words and dreams of the great Muhammad Ali, would have been null and void, full of nothing, but emptiness. You've got to back your dreams with actions! That is the only way to add substance to that which exists only in your mind.

> *"All men dream, but not equally. Those who dream by night in the dusty recesses of their minds, wake in the day to find that it was vanity: but the dreamers of the day are dangerous men, for they may act on their dreams with open eyes, to make them possible." – T. E. Lawrence.*

The Funding Lounge

1. List a specific reason why Business Credit might be beneficial to you?

_____

_____

_____

_____

2. How has having less than stellar (or down right awful) personal credit limited your firm's growth?

_____

_____

_____

_____

3. Does Business Credit appear to be a realistic options for you? Are you itching to get started building an amazing profile? If yes, what is the first step you plan to take?

_____

_____

_____

_____

"Always look for the fool in the deal. If you don't find one, it's you."
– Mark Cuban

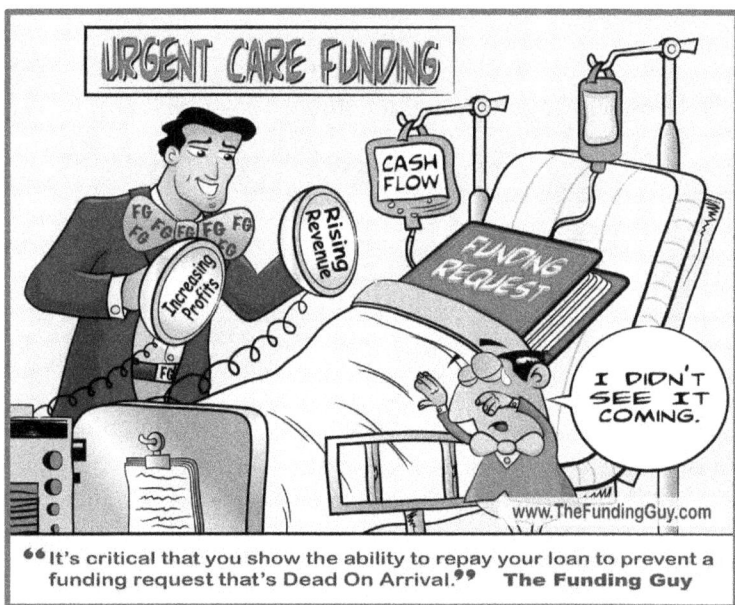

"The Funding Guy"

CHAPTER III

Stop Cooking the Books

t was salacious!

Rumors swirled that he had an accomplice on the inside. The tea leaves had to be true, right?

How else would a person not named Houdini be able to torture, maim, and murder (on the outside), while incarcerated and allegedly under 24 hour surveillance? The vile nature of his crimes made hardened criminals cringe and unflinching officers all surrendered their arrogance and began pleading for time off.

It was as if this guy was the boogieman.

Although housed 20 feet below ground in solitary confinement, the unrepentant miscreant, seemingly doubled down on his killing spree by taking out a sitting circuit court judge, the chief prosecutor, and a deviant who was already sitting on death row. It was as if this psycho was a master puppeteer, trying to show whoever was monitoring, him that he could pull a few strings, and "touch" whoever he wanted, whenever he wanted.

It was pretty baffling, no one could quite figure out how this smug, unapologetic serial killer was seamlessly executing the crime of the century - while in cuffs.

In a word, it was mind boggling!

Although this riveting tale sounds as if it was ripped straight from the headlines of the New York Post, this subplot is actually a snippet from my all-time favorite movie: Law Abiding Citizen, featuring Jamie Foxx as a hard-charging, unrelenting prosecutor, and Gerard Butler as a grieving husband, hell-bent on extracting revenge for the egregious murder of his wife and 8 year old daughter.

A huge movie buff, I'm like a kid in a candy store when executives at A&E or ION Television announce an upcoming 12, or if I'm lucky, 24-hour marathon of whodunit murder mysteries - featuring the likes of Law & Order, Criminal Minds, or 24 - starring my dude, Jack Bauer. I'd spend the next few days stocking up on juju beans, buttered caramel popcorn, and diet Sprite. Hey, hey, hey, open up your mind, the diet Sprite - helps balance out the calories.

In Law Abiding Citizen, Butler vows to take down a woefully incompetent justice system that sheepishly allowed his wife's killer to practically walk away free. This striking whodunit, ushers viewers through a series of twists and turns that would render a task force comprised of Lieutenant Colombo, MacGyver, and Detective Goren of Law & Order, woefully incompetent. If you said this riveting thriller was on par with the most captivating murder mysteries ever written, you would not get any argument from me.

What was most tantalizing was the fact that Butler's character didn't have access to the Internet, wasn't privy to a cell phone, and the keys to the vault were rightfully locked away. They had him right where they wanted him (or at least that's what they thought). It was surreal.

Despite their best-laid plans, Butler's murderous ways only intensified. The entire city was pulverized and shaken to its core. No one was immune! Kids didn't go to school. Mothers didn't leave their kid's side - except to sneak a peek at Scandal.

Adamant about quelling this monster's reign of terror, the mayor played by Viola Davis of ABC's: *"How To Get Away With Murder"*, threatened to give shotguns to every meter maid if that's what it took to rid the city of this monstrosity.

In a soliloquy from his cell, Butler's character, Clyde Shelton, calmly said:

> *"You see the body, you see the smoke - but the larger picture still eludes you."*

Everybody knew he was guilty of the carnage! Hell, he even unabashedly admitted to it. Yet he was essentially given the green light to exit court and carry on unscathed.

He continued his terror rant by saying *"unless there is any hard evidence against me, why are we here, why am I in this place?"*

The sadistic, egotistical maniac later pushed the envelope by vowing to ratchet things up to 'biblical portions' if his release wasn't imminent. Then, as if he was an appellate judge, the "catch me if you can" killer slapped Jaime Foxx's character with the most poignant line in this thriller: *"It's not what you know, it's what you can prove!"*

After listening to this line, I closed my eyes and imagined being back in one of my despicable loan committee meetings, where I was "gently admonished" by the Bank's president and his right-hand man (lender-friendly) for pitching deals that, in their words, were simply "smoke and mirrors."

Although I thought I had them right where I wanted them, (on the verge of funding my clients) they'd say the numbers were baffling!

No one could quite figure out how my smug and unapologetic clients were seamlessly executing the crime of the century - (COOKING THE BOOKS) then unabashedly applying for funding at our bank.

They repeatedly say, Magoo (As in the nearly blind cartoon character Mr. Magoo) could see the fuzzy numbers presented by my prospective borrowers didn't amount to a hill of beans. They said, "Son, enough of the pontificating! *It's not what you know; it's what you can prove!* Now go a-hunting, and fetch me a deal that shows a hint of profit or cash flow!"

It wasn't just me, no one was immune to their critical eye or sharp tongue. When the smoke cleared, and I moved on to greener pastures, I found myself to be a wittier, shrewder, more financially astute lender. So much so, that I was able to build a successful consulting practice, where I helped decipher fuzzy numbers, and coaxed deadbeats into becoming financial stalwarts.

Despite my best-laid plans, it was near impossible to slow the tide of rogue CPAs coaching their clients to recklessly hide their profits and cook their books. (Hence, my passion to pen this insightful book!)

Today, entrepreneurs are being shot down left and right; and failing miserably when approaching bankers for funding - due to smug, unapologetic financial advisors coaching them to pen their profits in disappearing ink!

Stunned? You shouldn't be!

For far too long, that's been the modus operandi, that has kept far too many entrepreneurs handcuffed and looking feeble when approaching Banker X.

Inexplicably, entrepreneurs are told its okay to write off everything from their weekly family groceries to their stylist appointments, pricey family vacations, and gourmet dinners. When that's not enough, they're told hurry, there's no time to waste, toss in every frivolous expense imaginable including; concert tickets, the kids daycare and the weekends at Grandma's.

In the blink of an eye, what was once a dynamic, highly profitable business on paper, morphs into a rag to worst horror story. Rather than being blown away, the banker is backing out, saying *"unless there is any hard evidence, why are we here? Why am I in this place?"*

Wealth Principle # 6

Tricks Are For Kids!
Wealth isn't built on double talk, or deception - but rather
dogged determination.

When informed that your business appears to be on its last leg, and funding is highly unlikely, you cry bloody murder. *You threaten to ratchet things up to biblical proportions*, then begin reciting the names of your A-list clients and exalting your connections to the bank's vice president; and affiliations with the mayor.

Incredulously these antics are all to no avail, as potential lenders are boiling over in laughter, thinking to themselves, are you serious? You have no cash flow, you show no profits, and so what makes you fancy you'll score a loan?

After scanning the funding proposal a second time, they check for cameras and ask, "*Am I being punked here?*" Barely keeping a straight face throughout, they bow out unapologetically, leaving the shattered entrepreneurs with two small cue cards.

The first read;

"It's not what you know, it's what you can prove."

The second says;

"You see the body, you see the smoke - but the larger picture still alludes you."

The larger picture for many disheartened entrepreneurs is that they run plenty of money through the bank for certain businesses, and a hell of a lot more under the table. However, because they bury profits so deep below the surface, it appears they can't afford to flick on the light switch or run water for more than 3 seconds without breaking the bank or racing to the court to file bankruptcy.

It's as if they're master puppeteers, trying to show whoever's monitoring their financials, that they can pull a few strings and spend whatever they want, whenever they want.

In their minds, everything is just peachy!

Unwittingly, by pulling this stunt they're announcing to every potential buyer or banker that it's probably best to walk away from their business. It says that your business is approaching stormy weather and leaking massive profits; kinda like the Exxon Valdez.

The problem, at least on paper, is that you're severely hemorrhaging cash and don't appear to be a viable candidate for funding or sale. Oblivious to the ramifications of sandbagging your books, you pat yourselves on the back and thank your lucky stars - you've been smart enough to avoid paying taxes for three consecutive years. You're thinking, what a brilliant financial caper. Meanwhile, your friendly neighborhood banker is pulverized thinking, *the larger picture still eludes you.*

I'm in your corner! I know its maddening having to fork over 3%, 33%, or at times what feels like 93% of your profits. This is especially troubling if you're like good old George Jefferson, finally up in the big leagues, and haven't had the luxury of really savoring your first piece of the pie. However, carrying three sets of books, one for Sallie Mae, one for Uncle Sam, and one for your shady financial advisor, can land the most unassuming book fixer in a tub of hot water. Unfazed by the heat in the kitchen, many stoke the flames by becoming a disciple of the little guy on TV who screams at the top of his lungs, *"Get your billion back America!"*

Bright eyed and bushy tailed, wannapreneurs adhere to his plea by sprinting to the nearest Family Dollar convenient store and having their taxes electronically prepared. The cashier (who doubles as a tax preparer) rings them up for their 75% off socks, half-gallon of discount milk, and a loaf of bread two days from expiring.

For the record, I'm the ultimate cheapskate, and as such, Family Dollar is one of my favorite shopping destinations, it really is. I'm actually ecstatic the discount grocer is popping up on every other corner in America. I'm simply of the opinion that talented entrepreneurs hoping to pitch their million dollar idea to a litany of bankers shouldn't be going to *The Family Dollar, The Family Pawn Shop or The Adams Family* to have their taxes prepared.

Playing this tainted game of moving the cheese isn't the savviest or most financially astute gesture by an entrepreneur looking to score millions in investments and working capital.

Wealth Principle # 7

Stop participating in your demise!
The people perished for they had no vision.

A Lot of aspiring business people are actually the architects of their own undoing, and they go about looking for who to blame. The Greek philosopher Plato once said;

> *"We can easily forgive a child who is afraid*
> *of the dark; the real tragedy of life is men*
> *who are afraid of the light." – Plato.*

Now that you've seen the light, I submit that in order to have bankers jostling to lend you growth capital, you absolutely have to stop masquerading like a financial lightweight. Your banker isn't Superman. They don't come equipped with X-Ray vision that enables them to see through your financial charade or bookkeeping shenanigans!

I can't imagine things working out too favorably once the underwriter sees your tax returns are signed off by Cashier # 0001, at Family Dollar.

Badda Bing!

Badda Boo!

You can kiss away hopes of landing working capital.

What many who are cooking or shrinking the books don't realize is that the nefarious game they're playing is a megaphone to the world that proclaims *"My business has absolutely no cash flow, no equity, no retained earnings, or for that matter, any ingredients worth mentioning!"* It whispers "my business isn't worth the cheap paper these horrid financials are written on!"

I submit that the fancy tax preparer you've employed is punking you. The once-mighty business you've had hopes of possibly taking public has metastasized into nothing more than a public mockery in banking circles.

- *I can't hold you prisoner and make you fix your books (if I did you'd probably escape anyway)*

- *I can't force you to show truer financial numbers or select a more financially prudent advisor, who'll straighten out the whodunit twist and point you to greener pastures.*

- *Nor can I rid you of the dirty little habit of COOKING THE BOOKS.*

However, if you want to live the life you've always imagined, one where bankers plant orchards of money trees in your backyard, then;

- *You've got to be brave enough to cut the fat - (frivolous expenses.)*

- *You've got to stop hiding profits in plain sight.*

- *You MUST and I mean MUST, cease and desist the practice of COOKING THE BOOKS.*

While it's entertaining for fictional serial killers like Clyde Shelton in Law Abiding Citizen to play - *hide and seek* - with authorities, it's highly unlikely you'll get away unscathed, when you're on the clock pitching to real life bankers.

This chapter isn't about me pointing the finger. It's not about the pot calling the kettle black, or about the glass being half empty or full! (Spin it any way you like)

It's about You, *The Aspiring Entrepreneur*, seeing the smoke, and not looking past it. It's about You, *The Burgeoning Business Person,* seeing the larger picture and building an amazing firm (on paper); one where bankers clearly see how profitable you are.

So, if you're committed to going organic - by that I mean showing your true numbers - you'll find a plethora of lenders giddy about escorting you to the cake and watching you eat it, too!

Wealth Principle # 8

Unless you're a Track Star,
Success isn't in the Sprint, it's in the Grind.

Slow and steady, they say, wins the race; you don't want to get caught up in the fast lane, when you don't really understand the rules of the game. You've started a business. You've worked your fingers to the bone. It's understandable that you might want to indulge in the finer things in life. However, taking short cuts and short changing your numbers on paper, is a recipe for failure. It great that you hustle, but hustle wise.

> *"Things may come to those who wait, but*
> *only the things left by those who hustle."*
> *– Abraham Lincoln.*

Before you throw caution to the wind and hurriedly bury your profits, decide whether you want to be A Law Abiding Citizen or rascal who's unwittingly digging their own ditch.

The Funding Lounge

1. List one way *COOKING THE BOOKS* can be detrimental to your funding search.

_____

_____

_____

_____

2. What corrective action are you prepared to take, in order to prove that your business is as dynamic ON PAPER as it is in real life?

_____

_____

_____

_____

3.) In Law Abiding Citizen, Clyde Shelton told the prosecutor *"It's not what you know . . . It's what you can prove."* What are your current financials saying to your banker?

_____

_____

_____

_____

"Yesterday's home runs don't win today's games."
– Babe Ruth

"The Funding Guy"

CHAPTER IV

Icing on the Cake

The idea was crippling! If you looked at him the way I did, you'd immediately join me in thinking, no way! Not him, never in a million years, not this dork!

How could he? Things didn't add up. The more I researched, the more it seemed like 1 + 1 = 11! I couldn't grasp how J. Wellington Wimpy, the burger-eating, zero cash carrying character, from Popeye The Sailor Man; was able to bait patron after patron at the Rough House Diner to cough up short term loans, simply by uttering his catchphrase: "*I'll gladly pay you Tuesday for a hamburger today!*"

Without fail, guest after guest, as if the Pied Piper hypnotized them, would dip into their wallet and gladly lend our portly pal, a few cents to purchase a super-sized burger with loads of pepper jack cheese, juicy pickles, and triple beef! I can't remember Wimpy ever ordering from the value menu. His philosophy must have been "go big, or go hungry." Without question, he was the envy of every Little Rascal in my neighborhood.

What a financial caper!

Whether it was his polished vocabulary, the Armani suit he sported, or the way he tipped his black fedora, Wimpy's words worked to perfection every time. Every time that is, except on the Tuesday, when it was time to make good on his oft-given promise to reimburse said patrons.

Surprisingly, the chicanery that allowed Wimpy to beg and borrow with impunity extended some 35 years. Eventually, the gig was up and he was forced to exit stage left to Mel's Diner. Unfortunately, many aspiring entrepreneurs have picked up right where Wimpy left off. The highlight of their week is donning a three button Versace, an elegant briefcase, and hightailing it from neighborhood bank-to-bank, soliciting funding for their burger joint or can't miss business venture.

Similar to Wimpy, they offer *smoke and mirrors*, by that I mean very little to hang their hat on. Like so many good intentioned entrepreneurs, they're full of hope and promise, but cough up very little in terms of reimbursement. To prove that they're financially astute, they brandish a 10,000-page business plan, cut and paste a fancy mission statement, then kick back and wait for their well-crafted plan to rake in piles of greenbacks. For good measure, they toss in a few glossy charts and fancy calculations – ripped from the seat of their pants. As clear as day, I see them grinning ear to ear, offering up atta boys, and patting themselves on their own back.

And why not?

They believe we're still in the "heyday of banking," the period from 2004 to 2007, when every banker they said "hey" to, was inclined to like and lend them money.

Boy, times have changed!

Although they've packed their bags and ostensibly all but abandoned small business lending, the ads bankers have pinned all over Pinterest and tweeted all over Twitter, insinuate they're still looking to dole out, *The Black Card,* and pump cash into every Tom, Dick, and Handyman's pocket.

If you believe that, I have a shiny little bridge, in a place called Brooklyn, I'd like to sell you! Take it from me a "quasi financial insider" that; today's bankers are really only in the business of making high, high, high, quality "LOANS" to individuals who demonstrate a strong propensity to repay the said loan!

They're no longer interested in skip tracing you to the moon and sky above, to retrieve their money. This is especially true after the *Great Recession*, where bankers lost their shirts, their shoes, and pot to scramble eggs. Yes, scramble eggs!

In order to avoid another financial fiasco and to keep what's in their safe, business lending has shifted from *Fast and Furious* to *Mission Impossible*, in the blink of an eye. While the tightening of business credit was designed to weed out the J. Wellington Wimpy types, the nuclear effect of this move has had, a chilling effect on the well-heeled and the Wimpy's alike.

Nowadays, unless you have the "It Factor" or you're carrying a genie in a bottle, winning growth capital appears to take an act of God! It doesn't matter how cozy you are, or how many times you've broken bread with your down-to-earth polished banker. It's highly unlikely they'd risk their livelihoods revealing insider secrets that'll give you the upper hand in negotiating and winning capital from their institution.

Lucky for you, I'm a fixer (á la Olivia Pope) who is willing to show you what excites lending committees, once they're behind the *Iron Curtain*; cherry picking the pros and cons of throwing the kitchen sink at you.

No need to duck for cover, - once I teach you the ins and outs of *Icing the Cake*, you'll have bankers rolling out the red carpet.

If you're excitedly thinking that this Robin Hood of Banking is going to don a cape and delve into a scholarly financial piece, I hate to disappoint you, it's not that type of party.

I'm still going half crazy - reminiscing about the 70 hour work weeks, constructing qualitative analysis charts for a plethora of fast food and healthcare acquisitions. So if you don't mind, I'll leave the Wall Street mumble jumble jargon about the price-to-earnings ratio, and internal rate of return, to the Bloomberg's and the Wall Street Journal "elite."

With apologies to the *uppity up* type, who'd rather side eye you and joke, "Oh you must be in the first rooow?" (Bob Uecker) I'm going with a slightly wittier, and far more practical approach to teaching the bedrock of credit, known as the **4C's of Credit**!

Stick with me . . .

If you'd "hypothetically", fallen asleep in Banking 101; like I did multiple times, your notes of the **4C's** may be almost as comically written as my own.

For that reason, let's review them quickly:

The first C, used to rule out potential borrowers, is **Collateral**. Essentially, collateral is what the banker can take from you in the event you default on your loan. If you have more than sufficient value in your collateral, kind hearted lenders might be willing to play Let's Make A Deal!

The second C is **Character**. Character is the Who, What, When and Where about the borrower. It asks; does the potential borrower have the requisite expertise to make this business not only work, but accelerate? Character also questions whether you possess a shady background or proved a gem in prior business relationships. It asks, has one always paid as agreed or do you have Tony, Big Frankie & Tiny, peeking through your windows seeking retribution for defaulted repayment?

It also asks; are you carrying too much or too little debt? Do you have a pristine record of repaying debt on time, or do you have a history of robbing Peter to pay Paulette - only when it's convenient for you?

The third C is for **Capital.** Capital asks, what do you have of tangible value to contribute to your project? Lenders aren't interested in sweat equity, or I'll gladly pay you promises. They simply want to know outside of your good looks and amazing grace, if you are bringing anything tangible to the table, i.e. building(s), fixtures, or equipment. They're trying to discern whether you have coins in the cookie jar, cash stuffed in the mattress or multiple sources of repayment in the event your business faces a sudden crisis. Essentially, what they're saying is, those bearing only sweat equity and dreams . . . Need Not Apply!

The final C is **Capacity**. Before the lender doles out the cheddar, they want to know with a high degree of certainty that their money is going to be repaid. Capacity asks whether you can comfortably make the payments on the loan you are requesting. Do you have a steady or verifiable source of cash that flows like clockwork? Do you have an annuity, a rich aunt, or a part-time job at Wally World to help out in the time of trouble?

While the aforementioned C's all play a pivotal role in the bestowing of working capital, I'm of the belief that *Capacity* is by far and away the most revered component of the lending tree. The problem that stymies far too many entrepreneurs is that they show up at their pitch session with Banker Bob, looking Wimpy!

By that I mean – talking loud and saying nothing!

- *Nothing is said about the origin of the "alleged" repayment.*

- *Nothing is offered as collateral, or as a show of good faith toward repayment.*

- *Nothing is said about the when's, the what's, and the how's of repayment.*

Everything offered up by the prospective borrower says, *"Colossal Waste of Time; All the World's A Stage; Performance of a Lifetime; Charlatan!"*

After a few minutes, the only thing the loan committee hears is blah, blah, blah, blah, blah, á la Charlie Brown, circa 1985!

Translation . . . another pie in the sky smoke and mirrors type, who is going to try and seal the deal with a Coke, a smile, and mythical Tuesday promise!

Wealth Principle # 9

Hope isn't a strategy!
Smoke and mirror isn't a go to move.

R ather than singing your praises, or the lyrics from the 50 Shades of Grey soundtrack, *"Earned It"* by The Weekend, that says;

"You're perfect

You're always worth it

And you deserve it"

Bankers are thinking hit the road Jack, while humming the lyrics of Vivian Green's hit, *Gotta Go!*

"I gotta go, I gotta leave,

So please don't make it hard for me!

I've gave enough, I'm tired,

I gotta let it go!"

When informed that their funding was killed in a "New York minute" *PretenPreneurs* go from brash and boastful to being infuriated and insulted. They ask the question; *who are they to judge me?*

Rather than greeting you with open arms and asking; how would you like your funding; paper or plastic? Lenders are left scratching their heads, and asking, "Where's the beef?" News flash: today's bankers don't have a craving for foolishness.

- *They aren't amused by childish game of hide and seek the assets.*

- *They aren't auditioning to be equity partners in your venture.*

- *They aren't interested in calculating burn rates, or sharing in the fruits of your labor 3 to 5 years down the line.*

They simply want what Wimpy wants, the beef! The more beef, the merrier! The beef, which I've referred to as the *Icing on the Cake* is a concise, step-by-step, plan that illustrates how you, the borrower; will repay the lender. Pie in the sky promises won't cut it here! The more the icing or sources of repayment you deliver, the faster and sweeter, your funding will be. End of story!

A quick demo of the *Icing on the Cake* principle is as follows:

Banker X: "Wimpy, how are you going to repay this short term loan?"

Wimpy: "I'm glad you asked. I have several verifiable sources of income which shows that I can easily make the $4,500 monthly note, for my new sandwich shop."

- *First, my current monthly profit for "Wimpy Subs" is $5,000 per month.*

- *Second, my retirement income from the Department of Correction is $4,000 per month.*

- *Third, I have $50,000 equity in my home. If necessary, I can tap it to make emergency payments.*

- *The Crème de la crème is my new military contract which kicks in; in less than 60 days. The monthly profit on that alone is $7,500.*

When you come bearing such delicious Icing, lenders become bright-eyed and bushy-tailed. Here's the thing, the real beauty of well-placed icing; is that, it can hide a multitude of sins.

The very banker you suspected of sandbagging your funding proposal and causing raindrops upon your head, will now turn a blind eye to credit warts and reclassify them, as minor indiscretions. The new tune they'll be singing will be strikingly similar to a guy who finds no fault in you.

- *Spotty payment history? I believe we can smooth things out.*

- *Convoluted business plan? It looks all good to me.*

- *Crumpled collateral? We'll reshape it.*

Talk about doing a 360 turn on the hallowed ***C's of Credit!*** In a heartbeat, bankers will go from world-class critic to congratulator!

Out of nowhere, the invitations to the country clubs begin rolling in along with the Al Green lyrics that say; *let's stay together*.

> *"I'm, I'm so in love with you,*
>
> *Whatever you want to do*
>
> *Is alright with me!"*

Whether it's the Fondu or the Strawberry flavored treats; *Icing on the Cake* is the great equalizer in lending. It ratchets up the excitement factor and turns, what was once, a rigid and nondescript funding pitch; into a show-stopping tasty treat!

The days of talking fast, stumbling over your words, and looking over your head, will be a thing of the past if you implement this principle.

What the Icing does, is change the entire tenor of the conversation from "I hope I can, I think I can" to "I can. I'm more than qualified for this loan, and the Icing – my multiple methods of repayment, clearly demonstrates that I'm one in a million and my business deserves millions."

Now that you've discovered the Icing on the Cake, the choice is yours. You can continue on like your cash-strapped Wimpy colleagues – indecisive, vague, dreamy, and in over your head; or you can turn heads by whipping up a little Icing and deftly applying it to your pitch. If you select the latter, I'm convinced lenders will be lining up to roll out the red carpet, tossing you the keys to the vault and smiling as they gleefully announce, "I'll gladly pay you Tuesday if you show a little icing today!"

Wealth Principle # 10

Develop A Billion Dollar Grind!
A minimum wage mindset will never foster excellence. Be so
good that they cringe at the thought off not being able to do
business with you!

The Funding Lounge

1. When you approached your banker in the past, were you more likely to timidly ASK for a loan or present a COMPELLING ARGUMENT on how you can easily repay said loan?

_____

_____

_____

_____

2. What specific ACTIONS can you take if you're going forward to alleviate lenders concerns, and to prove you're an ideal candidate for funding?

_____

_____

_____

_____

3. Which of the **4C's** is your weakest category? What action will you take to show repayment ability?

_____

_____

_____

_____

"If one does not know to which port one is sailing, no wind is favorable."
– Lucius Annaeus Seneca

www.TheFundingGuy.com

" View credit reports months prior to approaching your banker. Identify and resolve factors well in advance that might torpedo your funding request. **" The Funding Guy**

"The Funding Guy"

CHAPTER V

The Presentation: Is It A Teaser?

Presentation is priceless! Presentation is Priceless! Luck is what happens when preparation meets opportunity. These lines can be attributed to a number of great men in history, who learnt the importance of preparation.

> *"Making your way in the world today takes*
>
> *everything you've got. Taking a break from*
>
> *all your worries sure would help a lot.*
>
> *Wouldn't you like to get away?*
>
> *Sometimes you wanna go*
>
> *Where everybody knows your name,*
>
> *And yet they're always glad you came.*
>
> *You wanna be where you can see,*

The troubles are all the same.

You wanna be where everybody

Knows your name!"

I know I'm not the only one that loves this song! I see you just sitting there. I really do!

Stop trying to be cute, put down your double shot of Iced Vanilla Latte and join in! I get it, you're tone deaf - and the song, well it's a bit challenging. How about you just hum it then. I know you're smiling. Yeah, that's it!

If you're anything like me, you get goose bumps and begin tapping your fingers when listening to this timeless classic. It brings back so many memories: of Sam and Diane's on again-off again courtship. Carla's biting comments aimed at Woody and Cliff. Who can forget the cool-as-a-cucumber Frasier issuing up spill-your-drink, gut-busting humor. All the while, dueling back and forth with his (way to uptight stiff as a board) wife, Lilith!

After 28 Emmys, 11 seasons on air, and an average of get this - 26 million weekly viewers, Cheers is arguably the best sitcom that ever existed on television. With all the staggering accolades and feel-good memories Cheers aroused, the thing that forced me to race five blocks from the subway (briefcase in hand) and sprint up nine flights of stairs - were the jovial, over-the-top greetings Norm received at the beginning of every episode!

"Can we talk?" Would there really have been more than two and a half episodes, if it weren't for the whimsical Norm? Without fail, no matter what drama Dr. Frasier was trying to iron-out or hair-raising scheme Sam was embroiled in, the moment Norm stepped foot in the bar, everyone blindly erupted in cheers of *"Norm! Norm! Norm!"*

I can only imagine how safe, desired, and relevant Norm felt. He must have felt like the center of the universe. To be completely honest, I wanted to be Norm, or at least get what I'd coined *"The Norm Treatment."* Whether it was at church, at school, or in one of my recreation league basketball games, I lived for the moment the room would shudder and everyone excitedly screamed my name. I envisioned everyone – including the ones I owed money to - rising to the rafters, celebrating my entry into their presence.

In my mind, the only thing that could possibly eclipse that euphoric moment, might be a room full of stoic bankers. People who I've never laid eyes on, greeting me with high fives, excitedly saying, "We know your name, by the way, your approved mortgage papers are right this way!"

You're probably thinking to yourself this *Norm Treatment* is remarkably good, and you'd love to bottle whatever it is that Norm had. If those are your sentiments, then I'd like to let you in on a little secret. I've crafted an enticing way to get bankers to drop whatever they're doing and surrender their heart and passion to your pitch.

Not sure if your pitch needs an upgrade? Riddle me this? Is your presentation robbing or rewarding you?

If lenders are routinely dodging your calls rather than saying, "There's nowhere else I'd rather be," I suggest you throw sophistication and caution to the wind, grab a pen, and scribble down the keys to winning the *"Norm Treatment."*

Clearly understand this: you never get a second chance to make a first impression! If your cake is soggy, lopsided, saturated with gaping holes throughout, there's a pretty high probability that no one, and I mean no one, will be buying, whatever it is you're selling.

A Greek myth tells the story of a proud young man named Narcissus. Narcissus, loved himself to a fault. In his opinion, Narcissus, (yes, he referred to himself in the third person,) could do no wrong. He was God's gift to himself. He literally started his day, cheering his being. He was so infatuated with himself, that he detested those who loved him. Instead of reciprocating their affection, he fell in love with his own reflection in a small pond. For the life of him, he couldn't get out of his own way. Unable to take his eyes off his reflection in the rising tide-Narcissus drowned.

Today, is your ego causing you to drown financially? Are you unable to get out of your own way? Are you so full of yourself that you're failing to see the big picture? Here's the thing, when the person looking at the big picture, is your banker and they're eye balling a shabby funding package, you're immediately thought to be subpar or unworthy of their limited time!

- *No one will be cheering.*

- *No one will give your pitch the time of day.*

- *No one will want to know your name.*

Wealth Principle # 11

Be unbelievably prepared!
Be unquestionably appetizing!

Deliver a pitch that will make your potential clients grow two inches taller, rather than one that invites them to tremor and retreat.

Let me let you in on another little secret!

Today's *"Small Business Bankers"* - a fancy title for "yes men, and paper pushers" are for the most part glorified sales people who've been stripped of all their prior lending authority. Contrary to popular belief, neighborhood bankers are no longer considered banking royalty. Often times they're regulated to no more than order takers, akin to cashiers at your neighborhood fast food joint. In many instances, they're only authorized to fax your paperwork, shake your hand, and feed you a happy meal (a line of B.S.), while you sit and wait for a legitimate answer from the corporate big wigs. Sadly, they no longer have the luxury of gingerly holding your hand and polishing your paperwork, while escorting your funding request across the finished line. Nope! They're expecting perfect people with perfect paperwork on day one.

- *If you're stumbling out of the gate - by that I mean can't give the lender a breakdown on how the money will be used.*

- *Are you striking out looking - failing to bring all requested info?*

- *If you're still air balling free throws - lobbing pie in the sky projections.*

You appear less than financially astute.

As a matter of fact, you appear to be a Counterfeit CEO. Yeah I said it; *Instead of working the business, the business appears to be working you!*

Forget cheering you, or knowing your name, lenders will be nudging you to take your rag tag, half-baked,   bitter request, far away from their desk. Rather than singing your praises; more likely than not, the song they'll be singing will be Michael Jackson's *"Beat It"* where the second chorus says:

> *"Don't you ever come around here.*

> *Don't wanna see your face, you better disappear."*

> *The fires in their eyes and their words are really clear.*

> *So beat it, just beat it"*

You can scratch any insane rejoicing, or rolling out of the red carpet; in all likelihood lenders will be squirming in their seats saying: "I'm good! I'll pass!" As a matter of fact, they'll probably cordially invite you to exit the premises! Hoping for "*The Norm Treatment*" forget-about-it! (Said in my New York City, Italian accent)

Here's the deal, a funding request pitched sideways, piecemealed over a 3 week period and missing scores of documents, will undoubtedly get the return to sender stamp, in less than a nanosecond.

Nothing about your packaging says, Banker X:

- *I can comfortably repay this loan.*
- *All my ducks are in a row.*
- *I'm going to blow you away, once you lay your eyes on my jaw-dropping financials.*

NOOO! On the contrary, it tells your banker the only thing, they're going to get from you are; *Excuses, Delays* and a *Reprimand* from their "Chief Lending Officer" for presenting an ill-conceived funding proposal!

Aha, but the secret to winning an exciting audience with your banker; one where you have him or her wrapped around your finger, serving you hot tea and offering up the "Norm Treatment", is easier than you might imagine.

It begins with something I've coined the "*Executive Lending Summary.*" In 30 seconds, The Executive Lending Summary, cuts right through the mumble-jumble, stonewalling bankers, erect to keep you out of their inner circle and away from their bread! Once a lender snares a peak of your *Executive Lending Summary,* the tenor of the conversation dramatically shifts from; they have their hands out again; to right this way, I'll be delighted to handle your funding needs!

Forget having to prove your name, rank and serial number - you'll be immediately given carte blanche to name your price - and the terms of your funding.

How sweet is that?

Whether they're walking into a committee meeting, waiting at a red light or preparing to tee off on the 18th hole, they'll undoubtedly stop, stare and get excited about receiving your 30-second loan teaser! The beauty of a well-crafted *Executive Lending Summary* is that it'll have lenders crying out for you. Here's why!

- *It's concise*

- *It perfects your pitch*

- *It's only one page*

Your Juicy 30 second summary, addresses 95% of the questions a lender might have and excites 100% of the bankers that lay eyes on it.

You might say, that Lending Summary thing sounds like the greatest thing since sliced bread! From a lending perspective, truer words might never have been spoken. When you're in need of urgent funding, and can't afford to wait 7 minutes, 7 weeks, or 7 months to hear back from an overwhelmed lender, 9 times out of 10 this one-page love letter, does the trick.

This is particularly true, since all the relevant facts about your credit, cash flow, and business acumen, lay at your lender's fingertips! It's appetizing. It's exciting. It's Twitter for bankers.

Even if you're sporting less-than-perfect credit, lenders will be anxiously anticipating your full funding package. The finely-tuned *Executive Lending Summary* package tells bankers you're financially astute. It whispers in order to *WIN*, (let me repeat that) to *WIN* your business, they'll need to put their best foot forward and gift you a nice healthy piece of cake.

Wealth Principle # 12

Silence is Golden
But Execution is Priceless!

The period of waiting, silence or apprenticeship, as Robert Greene strongly advices; is a critical part of success. Every successful business person has to pass through the stage of silence, which is the period of learning and mastery, in this phase you must master the art of timing. Knowing when to launch out stands at the heart of success.

"He who knows when he can fight and when he cannot, will be victorious."
– Sun Tzu

The Funding Lounge

1. In your opinion what is the greatest benefit of having an Executive Lending Summary?

   _____
   _____
   _____
   _____

2. Describe one thing you can do that will have lenders itching to view your funding request?

   _____
   _____
   _____
   _____

3. What story is your current funding package telling bankers?

What story would you like it to quickly communicate?

   _____
   _____
   _____

4. What is the biggest thing holding you back from crafting an appetizing 30 second *Executive Lending Summary?*

   _____
   _____
   _____

*"Look, don't cry to give up! Cry to keep going.
Don't cry to quit! You're already in pain,
You're already hurt! Get a reward from it!"*
– Dr. Eric Thomas

SPREAD THE RISK

HEDGE YOUR RISK

TOO RISKY

www.TheFundingGuy.com

" Don't put all your eggs in one basket. Putting blind faith in a single lender to deliver the funding when time is of the essence is a recipe for failure. Connect with Multiple Specialty Lenders. " **The Funding Guy**

"The Funding Guy"

C H A P T E R VI

Spilled Eggs: The Conclusion

Stale breadcrumbs and just enough funding to fail, or countless bankers bearing gifts to solicit your business.

You decide which it's gonna be!

Many of you are thinking; is this it? You're likely saying cute story, decent presentation.

If you're like me; a novice in the kitchen, you might have even picked up a thing or two about baking brownies. If you're being completely honest, you're probably admonishing yourself for having wasted 120 minutes rehashing things you've known since you started in business ten years ago. If I were a fly on the wall, I'd probably hear you say, "I'm so over you, Mr. Funding Guy. I was done with you ten minutes into this darn book.

How is this nonsense going to lead to an abundance of bankers racing to my front door?

If I read the tea leaves correctly, I'd respond by saying; there are two types of people, reading this book.

The first type is the group of you who are extremely, hungry and excited about implementing the strategies laid out in this book.

The second is a frightening group, who I'd classify as "Know-It-Alls". You know the people always crying, Why Them and Not Me!

I was a Know-It-All.   I was a rising star in the financial world, and I knew it. By the time I was 19, I'd worked at some of the largest banks on Wall Street. Not bad for a kid raised in the Webster Housing Projects, in the South Bronx.

By twenty-one, I was awarded a financial internship, where I worked hand in hand with the CFO of one of the most coveted insurance companies in the world.   My job, crafting a new line of credit cards, for the ultra-wealthy - put me among the most esteemed bankers in the financial district.

By twenty-three, I was accepted into one of America's most prestigious Bank Executive Lending Programs.

A few short years later, I was teaching regional bank presidents in Atlanta, Tampa, Nashville and New York, how to underwrite and adequately fund small business loans.

By thirty, I started my own boutique-lending firm. What the banks couldn't finance or figure out, I easily won funding for!

I was a Know-It-All, and I was good at it. I was crafting solutions to the most difficult funding scenarios in my sleep. I was building an empire, akin to that of Marie Antoinette and King Louis XVI of France. I was *"The Magnificent One"*- or at least I thought I was!

It wasn't uncommon for clients to wine and dine me on their luxury yachts or private jets. I even branched out into real estate, accumulating blocks of investment properties with hopes of constructing multistory high-end condos. I envisioned myself as some sort of mini-Trump.

I seriously considered running for mayor of my city, and why not? Like many of you, I thought I had the *"Midas Touch."* I was Mr. $500 Million! I'd been invited to be a keynote speaker for 1,000 of the wealthiest African Americans in the nation. Billionaires, with a capital B, would be scribbling down notes of my talk and clinging to my every word.

Things couldn't be more perfect – until The Great Recession of 2007 – 08, which pulverized an economy that was humming on all cylinders.

 For the life of me, I couldn't figure out why anyone used the term Great! What was so great about tenants dodging you, bill collectors chasing you and people leaping out of their windows, dodging bankruptcies and humiliation?

The economy was in a horrific free-fall. Everything that could go wrong went terribly wrong! As they say, Murphy's Law was in full effect.

- *The empire that I had burnt the midnight oil creating, was slashed and burned overnight.*

- *The real estate market was plummeting.*

- *Cottages on the hill for which I paid a King's ransom for were now being auctioned off for pennies on the dollar.*

- *Historically low gas prices, once my saving grace, were now inching north of $4.00 a gallon.*

I clicked on the TV and cringed as comedian Chris Rock delivered a series of one-liners about owning a fleet of luxury vehicles, yet struggled to scrape together the coin, to filler-up.

I offered up a faint "he's hilarious" and laughed while I sat with my then-wife and children. In actuality, I was crying deep inside. In real life, I was struggling with whether to drop my last $3.75 on a loaf of bread or drown it in the tank of my luxury SUV. I couldn't score working capital for seasoned entrepreneurs. I even struggled scraping up the $7.99 to pay my Netflix bill to catch up on Olivia, Fitz, and Huck :(that's *Scandal*, for you non-TV watchers.)

The more I thought about it, the more I hated watching TV anyway. Green with envy, the show I arguably hated the most had to have been ABC's award winning venture capital show, Shark Tank, featuring Mr. Wonderful.

What was so wonderful about those supposed "expert financiers" anyway? I angrily trashed the show. What could Mark Cuban $3.2 Billion Net Worth, Daymond John $300 Million Net Worth and Barbara Corcoran $200 Million Net Worth, teach me about real estate investing and small business lending, that I didn't already know. In my mind, we were all contemporaries - minus my paltry bank account which constantly hovered in the red.

Everything was spiraling out of control!

I was in a dire situation.

There were no more happy anniversaries or happy birthdays, as there was very little bread. I was wallowing in a land of lack! The *coup de grace* was an astronomical drop in bank lending, my *bread and butter*. I prayed so hard for the fiasco to end; I was plummeting into a deep abyss, from which there'd be no escape. Things got hard, then they became unbearable.

I could no longer explain to my wife how we'd eat.

Here's the thing: everything I was instructing my vaulted business clients to execute, I failed to do myself.

- *I'd recommended for clients to diversify banking relationships.*

- *I'd warned against the dire straits of putting all of their golden eggs in one basket.*

- *I reminded them to polish or update their funding plan quarterly.*

I harped on the fact that *Cash Flow Is King* and in order to Win Capital, they'd have to clearly demonstrate *Repayment!*

Because I was a Know-It-All . . .

Because I was a *do as I say . . . not as I do*, type of big shot, I got caught with my proverbial pants down! Like millions of Americans, I too had my lines of credit shut off overnight. One moment I'm waiting for the cashier to say paper or plastic - the next, I was being escorted out the front door! So much for shopping, "Where Shopping was a Pleasure!"

- *My go to lending buddies got laid off.*

- *The financial institutions where I enjoyed favorite status were shut down by the FDIC.*

- *I found myself on the brink of bankruptcy.*

I went from 60 to zero seemingly overnight. When you're buying a luxury sports car, 0 to 60 is an incredible thing. However, when you go from owning 60 apartments to zero in a period of 16 months, you're no longer the sporty fella people want to dine with. I went from living the high life to living in my car. I had become one of the hard-luck, heart-wrenching stories I had listened to thousands of times.

I watched former interns who I trained, acquire more than $800 million in commercial property for pennies on the dollar; while I was living in the land of lack, spending nights in Walmart's well-lit parking lots.

- *No more fancy cars.*

- *No more mini mansions.*

- *No more private planes or afternoons spent yakking it up on luxury yachts.*

My new life was filled with misery and missed opportunities. There was no more celebrating!

There was *No More Cake* . . .

I was living off day old bread and leftovers. I was living worse off than my rent dodging tenants. My thoughts were, Wait! What? How is this possible?

In the blink of an eye, I'd gone from *Financial Prodigy* to the *Prodigal Son.* I was no longer a conqueror. I'd been conquered!

Lenders who were delivering hundreds of millions to my former buddies were turning a deaf ear and a blind eye, to my funding request. I pressed close to their gold-plated doors, hoping my now wealthy pals, would catch a glimpse of me and decide to throw me a bone or a few crumbs.

I declared . . . It's not enough to simply know! My daily cry was Lord:

Why THEM and not ME?

Why THEM and not ME?

Wealth Principle # 13

Become A Hater!
Hate to lose more than you love to win.

There was no more daily bread! On what should have been the biggest stage of my life, I was dying a slow painful death! (Kinda like Ali)

My dreams of Wall Street opening their purse string to back my planned $150 million Small Biz Equity Fund went up in flames. Everything was slipping away from me. I was despondent, I was drowning in a fist full of tears.

- *My wife left - No she really left.*

- *I couldn't afford to feed my beloved dog (Toffy) - a beautiful, white retriever with a chocolate patch over his left eye.*

- *Creditors came Fast and Furious.*

My low point, my low point, was the day my car was repossessed and I was forced to walk six and a half hours and 15 miles in a hurricane!

It was the most humbling experience of my life. I wanted to cry, but what good would it do? No one would care, they had bigger concerns.

Her name was *Hurricane Sandy*!

As I plodded through torrential rains, followed by 90-degree heat, followed by thunderstorms, followed by 95-degree heat, followed by frightening bolts of lightning that seemingly stalked me for miles.

A light clicked on.   It was me!

- *I was my causing my own storm.*

- *I'd locked myself into a grimy pond of mediocrity.*

- *It wasn't the economy as much as it was me.*

Mr. Know-It-All!

Wealth Principle # 14

Kick The T.O.P!
Eliminate narcissistic tendencies that boast you're breaming with; *Talent, Opportunity & Potential*. Simply Go To Work!

Coach Vince Lombardi, the most revered name in the annals of the NFL once famously said;

> *"The man on top of the mountain didn't*
> *fall there." – Vince Lombardi*

This inspiring verse left a lasting imprint during my Enlightenment. It said to me that my "*I Will*", had to be greater than my "*I Can*", and my "*I Can*" had to be greater than my "*IQ*". It said, in order to reach my peak I had to get off my high horse and get to climbing. I vowed to *do the Necessary* versus being a *naysayer and known expert*. I committed to living a purpose-filled life.

I shut down what was left of my once lucrative practice and for 16 months, I spent 70 hours a week re-tooling, retraining and crafting an amazing gateway for those like me, who are *persona non grata*, in the banking community!

I worked with the best minds in the lending industry to build a simplistic blueprint that makes the Know-It-All, actually look like a Know-It-All.

Even if you're on the rough side of the mountain, you no longer have to reside in your house of cards scraping by on crumbs. As Confucius, the revered Chinese philosopher once declared;

> *"A man is great not because he has not failed. A man is great because failure has not stopped him."* – *Confucius.*

Wealth Principle # 15

Outlive the pain!
Stumble to greatness if you must. Just don't quit!

Today, it's time to say goodbye to missed opportunities and misery! You no longer have to rob Peter to pay Paul, in order to make payroll.

The ink has been cast!

Everything you need to make your cake or delight your banker is now staring you in the face. You don't have to struggle or try to figure out things on your own. I've done all the heavy lifting for you. It's perfectly gifted wrapped, right here.

If you're stuck in a life you never imagined, a life where hard luck and hard money lenders have become the norm - the only thing required of you, is a little action. You've already endured the pain - why not enjoy the promise?

I'm not telling you that the water will be turned to wine overnight or that your cup will run over in the first 24 hours. We're not serving that type of Kool-Aid here!

What I am suggesting is that, once you've nailed the Juicy 30-second intro I've coined the *"Executive Lending Summary"* and added a blend of the tips I've shared:

- *Make It Finger Licking Good*

- *Sweeten The Pot*

- *Stop COOKING THE BOOKS*

- *Apply "A" Little Icing*

- *Make It "A" Teaser*

There'll be no more crying your heart out or dizzying pleas for day old bread. The backhanded cheers of *"Let Them Eat Cake"* will be in your rear view mirror.

Rather than being a constant participant in the hunger games, or at the receiving end of belittling glares at the gate of the castle, you'll be given the keys to the city and combination to the vault. With the right system in place, inaction and excuses will be a thing of the past. *"Execution will be worshipped,"*

– Dr. Eric Thomas.

The great Winston Churchill, once proclaimed;

> *"Success is not final; failure is not fatal: It is the courage to continue that counts."*
> *– Winston Churchill*

In no uncertain terms this quote - screamed out to me "You can't fall if you don't climb. And there's no joy in living your whole life on the ground."

Today I ask you; what is keeping you grounded? What's keeping you in your land of lack? Why are you casting your lot on day old bread and barren food lines?

Thanks to the treats laid out in this tasty book, you now have the expertise to build a tidy little bread castle on the hill; and a cellar stocked with the tastiest cakes in the kingdom.

Bon Appétit!

Wealth Principle # 16

You must have Faith in your Faith
And Doubt your Doubts

Throughout this book, we have seen that no one is capable of achieving greatness without being resolute, that is what the 'Ali way' teaches. You've got to proceed with a 'stubborn rigor', like Davinci and never second guess yourself.

> *"The ones who are crazy enough to think
> that they can change the world, are the
> ones who do." – Steve   Jobs*

Wealth Principle # 17

Think Big! Shed Doubts
Live by a creed that says success is inevitable!

If you look at history books, you will find out that the most successful people are those people who had an undying desire to succeed. The realm of success is governed by the rules of persistence and consistency, you'll wonder why Davinci's motto is: Ostinato Rigore which literally means Stubborn Rigor.

> *"Always bear in mind that your own resolution to succeed is more important than any other."* Abraham Lincoln.

You must have faith in your faith and doubt your doubts. Once your resolve for success becomes shaky, your chances at success becomes narrower. You've got to live by that creed, push through obstacles and remain steadfast. There is no greater enemy of success, than leaving the project half way; you've got to join the beginning with the end. Who says the road to success is an easy one? Sometimes you've got to do it the *Ali way,* you might have to endure some pain and setbacks; you have to keep moving forward.

> *"The biggest obstacle to wealth is fear.*
> *People are afraid to think big, but if you*
> *think small, you'll only achieve small*
> *things." – T. Harv Eker.*

The Funding Lounge

"Success is no accident. It is hard work,
perseverance, learning, studying, sacrifice,
and most of all, love of what you are
doing." – Pele

If you love what you're doing, but you're embarrassed your funding request is bordering on impossible, you've opened the right book.

If you're committed to walking into a financial institution, wielding a great deal of *Influence*, and *Authority*; the good news is that, we've got you covered!

I know you're busy running your existing business, so I've created a *done for You Template* that will propel the busiest executive to financial stardom.

The days of being stumped and confused about how to *Get Your Cake & Eat It* - are a thing of the past. Simply Logon to www.*thefundingguy.com* and join our community of small business owners who are putting their best foot forward and scoring loads of growth capital!

Our lending coaches are former bank executives who'll take your hand and walk you through the maze of funding options. No more skating on thin ice, fumbling around blindly or following little voices pointing the wrong direction to you.

Our suite of Online training courses will teach you how to wow conventional lenders, navigate through treacherous waters of peer-to-peer lending. You will be enlightened on how to score Business Credit, seemingly overnight.

Finally, if you're in need of a few brownie points, we'll give you, **The Works!** *The Works!* is our all new training course that shines the light on the tricks of the trade, it'll help you boost your personal credit scores by as much as *150* points in as little as *150* days.

About The Author

Edward E. Felder, Jr. a 20 year lending executive; is currently a principal at SupplierFunding.com a boutique finance firm that delivers private funding to small and emerging firms with lucrative corporate and government contracts.

Prior to founding his firm, Mr. Felder worked as a commercial lender for a number of leading banks including Bank of America, AmSouth Bank, Barnett Bank, Connecticut Mutual and Manufacturers Hanover Trust.

Since founding Supplier Funding Mr. Felder has originated nearly $750 million in commercial funding. His expertise includes underwriting technology firms, manufacturing businesses, healthcare, staffing and a wide variety of commercial real estate development projects.

Through his debut book "It's Money In The Bank: 7 Insider Tips To Financing Any Small Biz", his second book "Business Credit Made Ridiculously Simple" and his amazing Funding Guy cartoon series, Edward hopes to inspire, and teach millions of entrepreneurs how to Win Friends And Greatly Influence Their Bankers.

Wealth topics Felder addresses during radio interview include:

1. Let Them Eat Cake ... Why bankers don't give you the time of day.

2. How to go from being a sidebar ... to a celebrity in your lenders eyes!

3. 1 Secret to Winning OMG ... Funding!

4. One Powerful Tool to Outsmart Your Banker!

To learn more about Edward (The Funding Guy), or to invite him to be a speaker at your next event, I invite you to visit www.TheFundingGuy.com. Felder can be contacted directly at 813 245-3293 or at 2TheFundingGuy@Gmail.com

To Your Ever Increasing Wealth

The Funding Guy

The Robin Hood of Banking!

Pssst…let's stay connected!

www.Facebook.com/TheFundingGuy

www.Twitter.com/TheFundingGuy

www.YouTube.com/TheFundingGuy

www.TheFundingGuy.com

www.SupplierFunding.com